SCHIRMER'S LIBRARY
OF MUSICAL CLASSICS

Vol. 265

SONATINA ALBUM

A Collection of

Fifteen
Favorite Sonatinas

For the Piano

Edited and Fingered by

LUDWIG KLEE, LOUIS KOHLER,
and ADOLF RUTHARDT

G. SCHIRMER, *Inc.*

7777 W. BLUEMOUND RD. P.O. BOX 13819 MILWAUKEE, WI 53213

Contents.

Progressiv order of Sonatinas.

SONATINA.

Fingered and phrased by
LUDWIG KLEE.

Op. 20, No. 1.

FR. KUHLAU.

a) These small slurs indicate that the last bass-note in one measure should be carefully connected with the first bass-note in the next.

sf
p
cresc.
f
decresc.
pp
legato.
mf
p dolce.
cresc.
ff

Andante.
p dolce.
pp
pp
p
cresc.
f
dim.
p dolce.
pp
p
pp
p
Rondo.
Allegro.
p
f
legato.
sf
f
sf
f
sf
sf
sf
sf

p
legato.
sf
p
pp
cresc.
sf
p
pp
f
sf
dim.
p
rall.
a tempo.
poco a poco cresc.
p
f
sf
legato

legato.

cresc.

cresc.

a tempo.

p dolce. *poco a poco* *rall.*

cresc.

SONATINA.

Op. 20, No. 2.

Fingered and phrased by
LUDWIG KLEE.

FR. KUHLAU.

a)
sf
p dolce.
sf
f
dim.
p
f
p
f
poco a poco dim.
p
cresc.
ten.
sf
sf
ten.
sf
dim.
p cresc.
p
legato.
p. f risoluto.
p
cresc.
f
dim.
p.
cresc.
a)

dim.
legato.
cresc.
cresc.
dolce.
dolce.
cresc.

Adagio e sostenuto.
p con espress.
a)
cresc.
mf
p
pp
p
mf
dim.
a)

a) Strike the appoggiatura simultaneously with the accompaniment.

cresc. assai.
f
dim.
p
cresc.
p
p
cresc.
p
cresc.
p
cresc.
f cresc.
sf p
dim.
p
Ped.
f
p
f

cresc.
poco a poco cresc.
a)
dim.
poco a poco decresc.
dim.
a)

Fingered and phrased by
LUDWIG KLEE.
SONATINA.
Op. 20, No 3.
FR. KUHLAU.
Allegro con spirito.
3.
dim.
dolce.
poco a poco cresc.
dim.
ten.
dim.
ten.
1.

poco a poco cresc.
dim.
p con espress.
dim.
dolce.
cresc.

a) b) Strike the appoggiatura, *f*, simultaneously with the notes for the right hand, *d* and *a*. c)

p
f stacc.
p
f
p
p
cresc.
sf
p cresc.
f
ten.
sf
dim.
p
cresc.
sf
p
p
cresc.
sf
1.
p
2.
p
dim.
p
fp
fp
dim.
p
dim.
pp
Allegro Polacca.
p legato.
cresc.

dim.
p
mf
cresc.
dim.
p
p
mf
p
f
dim.
p
mf
cresc.
dim.
f
sf
sf
p

sf
f
sf
sf
p
f
dim.
p
f
dim.
p
cresc.
f
dim.
cresc.
p
mf
p
cresc.
dim.
p

f

dim.

p

cresc.

dim.

p dolce.

legato.

cresc.

dim.

cresc.

sf *f*

SONATINA.

Op. 55, Nº 1.

Fingered and phrased by
LUDWIG KLEE.

FR. KUHLAU.

*) Remark: These small slurs indicate that the last bass-note in one measure should be carefully connected with the first bass-note in the next.

dolce.
legato.
cresc.
dim.

Vivace.

poco a poco cresc.
dim.

espressivo.
dolce.
p legato.
p
p
sf
p
p
sf
mf
sf
f
sf
p
poco a poco cresc.
8
f
p
f
p
ff

SONATINA.

Op. 55, № 2.

Fingered and phrased by
LUDWIG KLEE.

FR. KUHLAU

*) Remark: These small slurs indicate that the last bass-note in one measure should be carefully connected with the first bass-note in the next.

Cantabile.
p
pp
legato.
p
pp
legato.
a)
b)
p
8
dim. e rit.
pp
Allegretto.
p scherz.
pp
legato.
p
pp
legato.
f
sf
f
sf
a)
b)

cresc.
legato.
a tempo.
rit.
dolce.
legato.
a)
cresc.
dolce.
legato.
cresc.
a)

cresc.

dim.

cresc.

dim.

dim.

a tempo.

cresc. e rit.

legato.

cresc.

legato.

cresc.

SONATINA.

Fingered and phrased by
LUDWIG KLEE.

Op. 55, Nº 3.

FR. KUHLAU.

*) **Remark:** These small slurs indicate that the last bass-note in one measure should be carefully connected with the first bass-note in the next.

dim.
cresc.
cresc.
Allegretto grazioso.
a)
a)

p
mf
p
mf
dim.
p
mf
p
pp
legato.
smorz.
p
pp
legato.
mf
cresc.

pp
legato.
mf
f
dim.
p
cresc.
sf

SONATINA.

Op. 36, Nº 1.

Spiritoso. M. CLEMENTI.

Andante.
dolce
cresc.
cresc.
dolce
dolce
Vivace

dimin.

SONATINA.

Op. 36, Nº 2.

Allegretto.

2.

cresc.
f
p
cresc.
f
Allegretto
dolce
legato
fz
p
fz
p
cresc.
f
dimin.
p
fz
p
fz
p
fz
p
fz
p

Allegro.
dolce
dimin.
p
cresc.
f

dimin.
dolce
dimin.
dimin.
cresc.
dimin.

SONATINA.

Op. 36, Nº 3.

dimin.
pp
f
p
cresc.
f
ff
dolce
cresc.
f
p
cresc.
f
p
cresc.
f

Un poco adagio
dolce
sf
p
cresc.
f
dimin.
p
dolce
cresc.
dimin.
p
Allegro
p
fz
p
fz
p
fz
fz
p
fz

p
cresc.
f
dimin.
p
pp
fz
p
fz
p
f
p
f

SONATINA.

Op. 36, No. 4.

p
f
ff
dimin.
p
f
fz
fz
p
fz
fz
dolce
fz
fz
f

Andante con espressione.
p
fz
cresc.
fz
fz
fz
p
fz
cresc.
f
dolce
dolce
p
dolce
cresc.
f
dolce
p
fz
cresc.
fz
fz
fz
p
pp
cresc.
dolce
cresc.
f
cresc.
f
ff

Rondo

Allegro vivace

Da Capo al Fine.

SONATINA.

Op. 36, Nº 5.

p
cresc.
fz
cresc.
f
fz
fz
p
cresc.
fz
f
fz
fz
ff
p
dolce

fz
f
dimin.
p
tr
cresc.

Air Suisse (Original.)
Allegro moderato.
dolce
pp
cresc.
f
p leggiero
f

p
rallent.
a tempo
dolce
pp
f
ff
p
dimin.
pp

Rondo
Allegro di molto
p
f
fz
p
cresc.
f
dimin.
p
f
f
p
cresc.
f
p
p
f
Fine

p
fz
cresc.
f
ff
dimin.
pp
D. C.

SONATINA.

Op. 36, Nº 6.

p
dolce.
fz
fz
fz
ff
p
cresc.
f

p
f
cresc.
f
p
cresc.
f
ff
dimin.
p
dolce.
fz
p
fz
p
fz
p
cresc.

f
ff
fz
p
dolce.
fz
fz
fz
ff
p
cresc.
f

Rondo.

Allegretto spiritoso

dimin.
p
dolce.
f
dolce.
f
D.C.

SONATINA.

JOS. HAYDN.

p
cresc.
fz
p
pp
f
p
f
p
f
p
f
p
f
p
f

p
f
fz
fz
fz
fz
fz
fz

Adagio. Tempo I.
p
fz
f
f
fz
fz
p
cresc.

p
pp
f
p
f
p
f
p
f
p
f
p
f
p
f
p
f
f

Adagio.
mf
p
f
p
f
f
p
p
f

mf
fz
fz
p
cresc.
f
p
f
p
f

Finale.
Allegro.

p
mf
ff
p
1.
2.
f
f

p
f
p
f
p
p
f

SONATA I

W. A. MOZART

Abbreviations: P. T., Principal Theme; S. T., Secondary Theme; Close; D., Development; Coda; M. T., Middle Theme.

Abkürzungen: HS. bedeutet Hauptsatz. SS. Seitensatz, SchlS. Schlusssatz, DS. Durchführungssatz. Anh. Anhang, MS. Mittelsatz.

Allegro (♩= 132)

a) mp

P.T.
HS.

p

cresc.

f

S.T.
SS

mp

b) tr

a) *mp (mezzo piano)* rather soft; viz., between *p* and *mf*

a) *mp (mezzo piano,* ziemlich schwach) bedeutet einen Grad von Tonstärke, welcher zwischen *p* und *mf* steht.

b)  Less skillful players may content themselves with the following execution: or:  or even with an inverted mordent.

Schwächere Spieler können sich mit folgender Ausführung begnügen: oder: oder auch mit einem Pralltriller.

a)
p
cresc.
sf
b)
f
Close
Schl S.
D.
DS.
For less skillful players:
für schwächere Spieler:

mp dolce
cresc.

S.T.
SS.
mp
p
tr
p
tr
mp
mf
p
cresc.
f
tr
Close
SchlS

Andante (♩= 60)
p cantabile
P.T.
IIS.
pp
cresc.
dimin.
mp
p
mf
mp
p
mp
cresc.
f
mp
cresc.
mf
p

p
pp
cresc.
cresc.
f
mf
p
p
pp
cresc.
f
mp
cresc.
mf
p

S.T.
SS.
cresc.
cresc.
mp
P.T.
HS.

dimin.
mp
p
mf
mp
mp
p
cresc.
cresc.
f
mf
Coda
Anh.
mp
p
p
pp
mf
mp
mf
dimin.
p
pp
f
mf
mf
mp
p
pp
p
pp

Rondo
Allegretto grazioso (♩ = 104)
P.T.
HS.
p
cresc.
mf
mp
cresc.
p
cresc.
a tempo
poco rit.
mf
M.T.
MS.
mp
cresc.
f
sempre forte

cresc.
P. T.
HS
cresc.
cresc.
cresc.
cresc.
cresc.
dimin.
cresc.
cresc.

SONATINA.

Op. 49, Nº 2.

L. van BEETHOVEN.

f
p
f
p
cresc.
f
p
f
p
cresc.

Tempo di Minuetto.

pp
p
mf
f
p
f
p